COLOURTOONZ

The Colouring Series

3

Published By

DISCOVERY PUBLISHING HOUSE PVT. LTD.

4383/4 - A, ANSARI ROAD, DARYA GANJ,
NEW DELHI - 110002 (INDIA)
TEL: +91-11-23279245 / 43596064 / 43596065
FAX: +91 - 11-23253475
E-MAIL: parul.wasan@gmail.com
info@discoverykidz.in
WEB: www.discoverykidz.in